Glam, Grace & Mercy 15 Day Devotional

Glam, Grace & Mercy

To the most amazing woman I know, My Mother. You are everything I wish to be and I thank God for choosing you for me. To my amazing children, everything I do is for you and although you may not understand all of my decisions, I pray that one day you'll look back and know that you are the center of my heart. To my supporters, your penthouse thought is God's basement idea. Never ever stop believing in the power of Jesus Christ. I love you.

•

If we find ourselves with a desire that nothing in this world can satisfy us, the only probable explanation is that we need more of Jesus.

glam·our

ˈglamər/

noun

The attractive or exciting quality that makes certain people or things seem appealing or special

Grace

\ˈgrās\

noun

A virtue coming from God

mer·cy

\ˈmər-sē\

noun

Benevolence, forgiveness and kindness or help given to people who are in very bad or desperate situations.

Foreword

Someone once said "If you want to make God laugh…tell Him your plans." Every time I sit back and ponder the plans I had for my life, and how none of them have played out the way I wanted, I can't help but chuckle a little bit and believe God laughs at me too. The older I get, the more I am grateful for my cancelled and failed plans, because they've allowed for some of the greatest moments of my life—and some of the most important moments of my life. As I was reading this book, I couldn't help but feel like Brie had some little hidden cameras in my life this whole time and that's how she was able write this. This book touched parts of me I didn't know existed as I thought I knew all of my sides, as well as parts of me I forgot existed, the parts of me which didn't always feel beautiful but I know them to be. This devotional is an incredibly balanced compilation of scriptures and encouragement for any person facing difficulty in life.

Glam, Grace, and Mercy is the perfect title for the contents of what you are about to read. The author, Brie Elise, my personal stylist does on the pages of this book exactly what she does for me with clothes. She takes you on a journey and gives you options that best fit your need at a given moment based on experience, and trial and error (trials that result and error). I found myself pondering my own choices in life. I found myself coming to terms with the fact that each and every choice I have made—good , bad, or indifferent have brought me to this place I'm at now. I found myself answering the questions she asks within the devotional and I, myself ended up being ministered to and encouraged for once instead of doing it to others. I know you're wondering "Well what exactly does the lady writing this foreword do and who does she minister too?" "How did she even connect with Brie?" and "Why should I read this book?" These are all great questions and I'm glad you asked. I'll answer them all for you.

I am exactly the things described here in the ensuing chapters. I am a testament to God's grace and mercy. I think I'm quite glamorous these days too, but that's beside the point. My name is Adara Butler, and I am a Christian inspirational speaker and preacher. Brie and I met by way of the very thing I do all day, everyday: ministering. Besides preaching in the house of God, I use my social media accounts to upload encouraging inspirational messages from the Word of God. I started out on *Instagram* and I've since then moved to other social platforms like Twitter, Periscope, and YouTube –the whole nine yards. Brie and I followed each other on Instagram and she became the answer to a prayer I was praying for a long, long time.

As I have mentioned, I use my social media accounts to minister and I have shared pieces of my life in my posts. I openly talk about my story of redemption, identity, purpose and peace. I grew up in a devout Christian home, I attended church but wasn't always attentive to what was taught in church or my home. I strayed away much like the prodigal son did in the bible and I became a prodigal princess. However, no matter how far we go, God's grace is sufficient and meets our every need. I was a sinner who needed saving and God was gracious and mindful enough of me to save me. I share my story of redemption everywhere I can and it just so happens that Brie came across my page one day. As Believers we don't believe in fate or coincidence, so we know that was God's doing. She stumbled upon my account for encouragement but little did she know she was placed in my path to help me as well.

She was the answer to my prayer. I came from a lifestyle of partying, "turning up" and less than classy behavior and modest attire. The hardest part of the change from somewhat "ratchet" to righteous was rooted in my stance of not wanting to be a frumpy preacher. I wanted to look fashionable and preach the word of God. I am of the conviction you can be a woman of God and dress tastefully. You don't have to walk around in a burlap sap to prove you are holy. So, I wanted to be stylish and classy, but still saved. The problem was I didn't know how. Everything I had was either so super old looking to me or too provocative of a woman who claimed to be holy and set apart. I prayed for God to point me in the direction of someone who could help me elevate my wardrobe and still look tasteful.

You know what they say….be careful what you ask for right? I got just that. I got a personal stylist who not only is a Christian; she was able to relate to where I came from and understood where I was headed. She styled me once and from that event we began a friendship and working relationship. She shared with me bits and pieces of her life and what glamour and style meant to her and it just clicked. Brie was placed in my life to minister to me as I was to do the same for her.

Glam, Grace, and Mercy is extremely timely and significant for the person perhaps who is trying to find their way. I mean, we all are searching for something. Whether its identity, peace, belonging, love, or forgiveness—we

ALL are on a search. In her book, she shares her bouts with these searches and gives you a chance to reflect on your own possible personal encounters with these. Using very personal examples from her childhood to adult years she tugs at your heartstrings and makes you think about life and even the "blessings of the thorns" in our lives.

As an author myself, I can say writing a book is not as easy as people think it is. It takes dedication, time, love for the subject and passion for which the book is written. You can be sure you find all of these and more within the pages of this short, but powerful book. I believe everyone anyone can be motivated and captivated by this book. A person trying to make sense of events surrounding family issues, broken relationships, and self esteem indefinitely could use an inspirational read such as this. This book does an exceptional job for empowering its reader to revisit experiences for the sole purpose of becoming a better person from them. Coming from an extremely gracious and glamorous woman of God, I can confidently say *Glam Grace, and Mercy* is a perfect read for people of all ages. You will enjoy and be blessed by it. I know this because I was. I would read it again and recommend it to all my friends. Cheers to wonderful books, wonderful authors behind them and all the even more wonderful people who will enjoy this. God bless you.

Minister Adara L. Butler
Author of *A Prodigal Princess*
New York, USA
www.adarraaa.com

Glam, Grace & Mercy

On the following page, I've provided a mini prayer journal. You'll find this page throughout the book. I encourage you to utilize it during this devotional. Memory verse is a spot for any verse you would like to memorize on any topic. Prayer and Thanksgiving is a simple way to acknowledge the goodness of Jesus Christ in your life and the life of those around you. If we can't be thankful for others blessings, then how can we truly practice gratefulness to God? Confessions are the acknowledgement that we are guilty of a sin. When we confess to Jesus, we are admitting our wrongdoings and making it clear with our words that we are sorry and ready for change.

Today is: _____

Memory Verse or Inspirational Scripture:	Prayer and Thanksgiving for Myself:
My Confessions:	Prayers for Others:

My story is quite different from anything I've ever heard before. I was born to a mother who was extremely young. Her mother was pregnant at the same time, so they came to a mutual decision to put me up for adoption. The town I was born in was predominately white, so I was sent to a Memphis adoption agency/orphanage. This gave me a chance to be adopted faster, because at that time many Caucasians weren't looking to adopt a black baby. When I was born my mother opted to not see me, hold me or make any contact with me. She felt she would become attached and she would form a connection that would be hard to break.

My adoption was finalized on June 27, 1988. My original birth certificate was replaced with an amended one with my mother's (when I say mother I'm speaking of my adoptive mother) name on it. My records were sealed and my life went on. The only thing I know of my biological family is that my mother was around 5'6, brown skinned and into the arts. My biological father was supportive of her decision.

Most adopted people that I've met know quite a lot about their biological family, which has always left me curious, angry and confused. It's hard knowing who you are when you don't truly know anything about yourself or your biological family. As we speak, I'm searching high and low for information about my birth family. My goal is to thank her for such a selfless act. God knew exactly who and what I needed in this thing called life. She has no idea how her decision impacted me in such positive ways. Only God knew that her decision would eventually impact hundreds of people. This book is about my journey to finding myself, love and hope for the future.

I've created a collection of devotionals and short stories from events in my life. I pray that in the end you'll take my examples; good and bad, and apply them to your life in order to overcome any obstacle God tests you with.

DAY ONE

Lessons from Not Knowing Who I Was

There was never really a correct way to ask God why, but there were so many times, I really needed the answers. With brown eyes, cheekbones as high as the Eiffel Tower. teeth slanted, yet straight and brows as bushy as the tail of a rabbit, I'd always wonder; "who am I and who do I look like?" As I stared at the face that was so familiar, yet still so unfamiliar to me. I asked myself; "how can I love myself when I don't even know who I am? I walked through the halls of buildings, and looked into melanin rich faces and I wondered if I came from the womb of the woman who said hello to me. I'd lie in bed and wonder if this was really life. Am I dreaming or is this reality? How could my own mother give me away? I walked through crowded rooms and stores, and thought if there was another face in the crowd that looked like mine. I'd go through the checkout line of a clothing store and wonder if this person could possibly be related to me. I'd go to the doctor's office and leave my family medical history blank, because I had no idea about any of it. I always felt loved by my mom, but there was always something missing. And for years I thought that, that missing piece was my biological family. I was adopted at 3 weeks old. My biological mother and my maternal grandmother were pregnant at the same time and chose the other baby over me. I've never met anyone who has the same blood running through their veins as I do. I can't ever remember not knowing that I was adopted and thankfully nobody in my family ever treated me bad or any differently. Frankly, I'm convinced many of my family members have no idea I'm adopted. I just didn't understand how someone could give away their own child and never even look for them. I resented her for that. I would sit and day dream every day about meeting her, but then the thoughts in my head would become negative.

Reality set in, when I realized I was designed just for the woman I was with; my mother. Genetics could not have been more unnecessary. God could not have been more precise, when he allowed a 33-year-old, single black woman, with poise and grace, to pick me out of a room full of babies. She picked me. I picked her. God put us together. Although, I thought I was missing what it felt like to know someone blood related to me, I wasn't missing anything at all. People always say blood is thicker than water, but for me, that couldn't be more false. The blood of Jesus was better than anything and he knew exactly what a little chocolate baby born in 1988 needed. I've always had family. I learned at a very young age that family had nothing to do with blood. Family consisted of the people who loved you unconditionally. I love to think of the story of Moses when it comes to my adoption. Moses was adopted by Pharaoh's daughter, yet regardless of where he came from, he had such great purpose. God planted purpose inside of him from the moment he came into the world. God is so intentional with all that he does.

In order for me to heal from my past, I had to learn to forgive. I had to learn the true meaning of forgiveness. How could I love myself, while torturing myself at the same time? How could I look at myself in the mirror, knowing my face looked like the woman who gave birth to me, without even realizing she made the best decision in the world for me? I was destined for this. I was destined to learn the art of forgiveness no matter how many times God had to show me the lesson in the midst of the debris of life.

In the early stages of my life I was diagnosed with a rare disease called Recurrent Respiratory Papillomatosis (RRP). This is a disease in which tumors grow in the air passages leading from the nose and mouth into the lungs. In many cases the tumors grow back even after they are surgically removed. This has been a constant battle in my life. I've had well over 100 surgeries. By the time I was 4, I had a trache. The hospital was my second home and nurses and doctors were my second family. The person who was by my side the entire time was my mother. She could have easily given up on me, but instead she prayed over me and loved me unconditionally.

My mother is awesome. I can't imagine calling anyone else mom or being as close to anyone else. I remember watching a movie with her and during the movie, a princess had to be kissed by her one true love in order for a spell to be broken. The princess was kissed by someone she considered her mother and the spell was broken. It warms my heart to know that so many times we forget the true love can come from anywhere, as long as it's agape love. The love that Jesus Christ has for his kingdom is the kind of love that's true. After watching the movie, my mom quietly mentioned that I was her true love. From the day she met me, she knew that I was her daughter. With that, I am so content in knowing that family has absolutely nothing to do with blood. Family comes from the bonds we form with people who love us unconditionally. I was so busy looking for what I was missing, that I didn't even notice how blessed I was. His plans for our lives never fail. Even in the midst of our confusion, He is setting up so

many blessings and breakthroughs. I had to learn that I AM
WHO GOD SAYS I AM.

Moses: From Adopted to Deliverer

Scripture Reading:

Exodus 2:10 (NIV)

*When the child grew older, she took him to Pharaoh's
daughter and he became her son. She named him Moses,
saying, "I drew him out of the water."*

Devotional Reading:

Through different seasons of life, people work hard
to "find themselves." God has created us so that we need to
know who we are; where we come from; how we got to
where we are; and where we are going. If any of these
questions are left unanswered in our lives, we tend to
struggle with finding our identity and understanding the
"me" on the inside. Those people who have been adopted
experience these kinds of struggles even more. Not
knowing or not having a significant connection to our
biological parents can lead to an identity crisis in our lives.
But, God is able to take that identity crisis and turn it in to a

character growing episode. That is exactly what the Lord did with Moses.

Moses was adopted. Rather than lose her son to Pharaoh's edict, Moses' mom set her infant boy adrift in the Nile where he was discovered by Pharaoh's daughter. Though Moses' mom had the privilege of caring for and feeding the newborn Moses during his early months, when Moses grew older, he went to live in Pharaoh's house and was raised by Pharaoh's daughter. As stated, Moses was adopted.

At least partly because of his struggles with his identity, Moses had compassion for the Hebrews (because he knew them to be "his people") while still enjoying the luxuries of living in Pharaoh's house. This tension eventually exploded when Moses saw an Egyptian mistreating a Hebrew, lost his temper, and killed the Egyptian. After the event was discovered, Moses was on the run. For forty years, Moses wandered the wilderness eventually marrying, having a family, and tending a flock. But, this man who struggled with his identity, his nationality, his adopted family, and now his life in hiding was called by God through the burning bush to return to Egypt and become the great deliverer. The one that God would use to rescue the Hebrew people from slavery (see Exodus 3).

After leading the Hebrew nation from Egypt to the border of the Promised Land (by way of a 40-year detour through the desert), Moses had accomplished what God wanted him to do. Though he was adopted and struggled with answering the question "who am I," God eventually called Moses to be a great leader. Moses worked out his internal battles and through obedience put himself in a place to be used of God.

Maybe you were adopted, too. Maybe you have struggled with the "who am I" question as a result of that. Hear this: God knows exactly who you are and what He wants to do in your life. God wants to use you to make a great impact for His kingdom. Being adopted doesn't disqualify you from doing great things for God. In fact, it may just be what God uses to prepare you for the greatest journey of your life, hearing and answering His call. That's what God did through Moses, though he was adopted. God can do that through you, too. Let Him!

Devotional Questions

1. Have you ever felt like you were wandering through the wilderness?

_____

_____

_____

_____

_____

_____

_____

2. What eventually brought you out of the wilderness? If you still feel like you're in the wilderness, why do you feel this way?

_____

_____

_____

_____

_____

_____

_____

_____

3. Fitting in is something many people try to do, but we are called to be set apart. What has happened in your life that has shown you that you are set apart and/or different from the world?

_____

_____

_____

_____

_____

_____

_____

_____

_____

_____

_____

_____

Today is: _____

Memory Verse or Inspirational Scripture:	Prayer and Thanksgiving for Myself:
My Confessions:	Prayers for Others:

Day TWO

Forgiveness

Glam, grace and mercy....three absolutely beautiful words with even more beautiful definitions. Descriptions of my life and how far I've come, but if you knew of my dirty past, you'd question how in the world those three words could even describe a woman like me. 3 out of 10 teens will become pregnant at least once by the age of 20 years old. 25% of those teenagers will become pregnant with a second child within 24 months of their first birth. 1 in 5 girls is a victim of child sexual abuse. Teen mothers will most likely develop a feeling of worthlessness, low self-esteem and an abnormal or distorted view of life. I was that teen mother with the distorted view of life. I was the one many people wrote off.

As I laid in the middle of my driveway, I had no idea why I was allowing this to happen to me. I had been drug out of my house, down concrete steps and pushed and shoved down the driveway. I was tired of being hit, I was tired of being lied to, I was tired of growing up too fast, but it was too late. I was tired of being unhappy, but I didn't know who else would love me. At the time I had no idea what love was. What is love? "He only hits me when I make him mad."

These were the thoughts of a 15 year old girl, making excuses for a boy who abused her. I was hiding a pregnancy and I was afraid. I was so eager to prove everyone wrong. I wanted a high school sweetheart, just like the girls who talked about me at school. I wanted the seemingly picture perfect fairytale. Why wasn't I good enough?

I compromised my standards for nothing.

I remember a huge storm one night. My mother and I were having a disagreement and I decided to leave the house with my daughter. I literally ran away in the middle of a thunderstorm. Strange men stopped their cars and asked if I needed a ride. Terrified…I said no. I really wanted to go back home. My boyfriend never came to rescue me. Nobody came. I got a phone call from my grandmother, begging me to go back home. She said I was hurting my mother. I was so confused, hurt and humiliated. I ran away with my child for nothing. I ran away from the love of my family for a boy who called me everything but my God-given name. I ran away for a family who treated me like an animal and told me I would never be anything in life. I can still remember getting a phone call from his mother. She told me I was stupid and I was trying to trap her son. She told me I would never amount to anything and that I was faking my pregnancy. I had never been so humiliated in my life.

I remember writing him a letter and asking him to stop hitting me. He never responded. I remember praying that God would make my situation disappear. It didn't. I remember being dragged by my collar across a hallway and begging for him to stop. He finally did. After giving birth to not one, but two children by the time I was 17, I believe God was screaming at me to stop. They saved me. God saved me. Why couldn't I see that the love I was searching for was already within me?

I woke up one day and decided to make a decision. I felt trapped. I needed to go somewhere and change my life. I needed to be away from him. Away from the city I grew up in. I needed to go to college. My family was supportive, so I did just that. It was the start of a new beginning, but I had no idea how to forgive myself and I felt like I was too dirty to cling to Jesus. I desperately needed to forgive myself and repent for my past actions.

Scripture Reading:

Matthew 6:14-15

"[14]For if you forgive other people when they sin against you, your heavenly Father will also forgive you. [15]But if you do not forgive others their sins, your Father will not forgive your sins."

Devotional Reading:

Cancer is an ugly disease. What starts out as a few mutated cells becomes a dangerous disease as the messed-up cells replicate and spread throughout an organ and possibly throughout the entire body. Lack of forgiveness is the cancer of the soul. What starts out as an unwillingness to show grace to someone spreads throughout the soul; to impact a Christian's relationships with others and walk with the Lord. Left unchecked, refusing to forgive can be just as deadly to our soul as cancer is to our body.

Matthew 5, 6, and 7 make up the Sermon on the Mount where Jesus teaches what Kingdom living looks like. Jesus lays out the expectations for what it means to be living for God in this world. One of those expectations is that we will forgive others when they wrong us. But, just because Jesus instructs us to forgive does not mean that it is easy. Forgiveness is hard because someone has hurt us. And the deeper the hurt, the more difficult it is to forgive. But, our call to forgive is not based on the severity of the wrong done to us. Jesus does not qualify our forgiveness on a scale that depends on how big the action was against us. We are called to forgive the little stuff and the big stuff – the easy to forgive and the hard to forgive.

Forgiveness does not grow out of our ability to forgive as much as it grows out of our realization of how much God has forgiven us. When I realize the pile of sin that I have been forgiven, my attitude is in a better place to forgive others. When I see how much my sin breaks the heart of God, but He forgives me anyway. I am better able to forgive someone else who has hurt me and broken my heart.

Forgiveness is not given because the person deserves to be forgiven. Instead, forgiven is extended because the person does not deserve it, but we can show grace to them. If they deserved it, it would not be grace showing forgiveness but duty showing obligation.

How can we forgive like that? Did not God extend to us that same kind of grace showing forgiveness that we did not deserve? The better question is: In light of all that God has forgiven me for, how can I not offer a similar grace of forgiveness to someone else who has sinned against me?

God is so insistent that I forgive because He ultimately knows that when I don't forgive, I am the only person that is hurt by that choice. Typically, the people I am refusing to forgive either doesn't know or doesn't care that I have not forgiven them. They are not carrying that around every moment of every day. But, I am. Forgiveness frees me from anger and bitterness.

God showed us how to forgive. Then, Jesus called us to forgive. Now, the only option is to choose to forgive. Who do you know that you need to forgive?

Devotional Questions

1. **Who or what situation are you NOT forgiving and why?**

_____

_____

_____

_____

_____

_____

_____

_____

_____

_____

_____

_____

2. Do you hold grudges and why?

_____

_____

_____

_____

_____

_____

_____

_____

_____

_____

3. Research and find 2 bible verses to meditate on that discuss forgiveness.

_____

_____

_____

_____

Today is: _____

Memory Verse or Inspirational Scripture:	Prayer and Thanksgiving for Myself:
My Confessions:	Prayers for Others:

Day THREE

Power to Forgive

Sometimes you have to learn to stop holding on to mistakes, just because you spent so many years making them. When I was 16 and pregnant, my children's father was denying my existence and slandering my name. I hadn't been with anyone else but him, yet I had to face the results of my own ignorance. To this day I still remember the phone call when their paternal grandmother called me up one day and told me I was just using a pregnancy to get what they had. She said I would never be anything in life and that I was stupid. Today, my children are 10 & 12 and if their paternal side of the family were to walk past, they wouldn't even recognize them. I was never the type to do crazy things or force anyone in my life, so I moved on with my life and never looked back.

I repented to the Lord and asked him to forgive me for my part in the mess of my life. I desperately needed closure from the Lord and I needed his forgiveness in order to fully be restored from my past. Once I let go and let God, my entire life made a 360. I am a completely different person and my life is more different than ever before. Back then, I would have never imagined having a life as wonderful and blessed as I do now. Today my children are extremely smart, well-mannered and they want for nothing.

I went on to finish college and graduate school. I have multiple degrees. I rededicated my life to Christ and I was blessed to have an awesome career. I became a business owner and was signed to a popular modeling agency here in Memphis. I was at my job one day and I walked in on an older lady mopping the bathroom floor. That lady was my children's grandmother. This was the same woman who called me derogatory names and told me I would never be anything. I could have easily made a smart remark or insulted her, but I didn't. My heart started to flutter, my stomach turned and all the memories of how painful she made my life came back to me. But I didn't have anything negative to do or say. I looked at her and simply said hello. She looked like she saw a ghost and held her head down. I just walked away and moved on. Previously, I thought about all the things I would do and say if I ever saw her, but that was many years ago. This time I didn't feel any anger or bitterness towards her, but I realized I finally had forgiven her. I said all this to say, God's revenge is best. He will literally make your enemies your footstool. He will put you in a position where your enemies will have no choice but to see you succeed. I forgive her. I forgive him. I forgive them.

I have moved on. It took so much energy to hold a grudge. Holding on to pain takes way too much time and effort and quite frankly its hypocritical to think we are worthy of the Lord forgiving us, when we can't forgive others.

Scripture Reading:

Acts 3:19

"Repent, then, and turn to God, so that your sins may be wiped out, that times of refreshing may come from the Lord"

Devotional Reading:

T.G.I.F (Thank God I'm Forgiven!)

There are some situations where the people who have hurt you don't realize the pain they have caused in your life. We often spend days hoping for an apology that just may never come. In order to expect others to forgive us, we must be able to forgive our part in situation and rent. Repentance doesn't mean going through life beating yourself up about what you did. It means that we confess to God our wrongdoings and ask God for forgiveness and start doing the things that please the Lord and not our flesh. Start practicing what you believe in. Practice how you would want others to treat you in situations. Love others the way Jesus loves us.

The word "Repent" means that as Christians we feel or express sincere regret or remorse about our wrongdoings or sin and we start doing the things that we know we should do in Jesus name. If you are alienated from somebody, be reconciled. (Please note: Reconciliation does not mean restoring a broken relationship or going back into a situation that God has purposely removed you from). If you are self-righteous when it comes to others, humble yourself. If you have been uncaring toward those who are in need, now is the time to gain morals and put yourself in the shoes of another human being. Repentance is not some negative, life-denying gesture. In fact, repentance doesn't mean turning to a past way of thinking or doing at all. Repentance means turning to a new way. Repentance does not mean to change from what we are to what we were. It means to change from what we are to what we are going to be."

Devotional Questions

1. **Write a letter to the person you haven't forgiven, pray over it and give it to them or destroy it. This is a representation of letting go of the pain and unforgiveness you've been holding on to.**

Today is: _____

Memory Verse or Inspirational Scripture:	Prayer and Thanksgiving for Myself:
My Confessions:	Prayers for Others:

Day FOUR

God's Plans for Your Life

Recurrent Respiratory Papillomatosis is a disease that often leads to death. Doctors told my mother I wouldn't live to see the age of five. If I did live, I would need to learn sign language and would never be able to speak. As I write this book, I am a 28 year old mother of two. I hold a Bachelor's Degree in Nutrition and Dietetics, a Masters in Public Health and a certification in Healthcare Management. I work for an amazing company and I've accomplished everything I've put my mind to. I can't say that any of this was easy, but I worked hard and God made a way. When God has plans for you, it doesn't matter what you're diagnosed with, what you may think you lack, your baggage or what society says about you. He has equipped you to win, if you allow Him to lead.

Let me be clear, nothing has been easy. It's been an absolute beautiful mess of a struggle. After I received my Bachelor's Degree, I was working at Sears. Yes, I spent 5; not 4 years, getting a degree in an awesome major, only to be working somewhere I could have worked without a degree. I was devastated. I felt like a failure. Prior to getting the job, I spent most of my summer attempting to find work. I sent countless emails, revised tons of resumes, applied on every job on Indeed and made about 20 different cover letters. I perfected the art of interviewing. I created a Pinterest account and "pinned" hundreds of pins on how to get a job and how to blow companies away during interviews.

I felt pitiful and pathetic. I would mope around literally in tears. I remember my mother sat me down one day and showed me her salary from the time she left college up until now. She started off literally making pennies. When I think of it, I can't even fathom how she survived on her own back then, but now she is extremely successful and if I could ever dream up the perfect role model, she would be it. The talk made me feel better, but my job-seeking failures made me feel like a failure. When was it going to be my turn? God…don't you see how faithful I've been to you? Faith without works is dead. I worked…so why does my life feel dead? What was God waiting for? Where was my future, my happiness and my hope? And why was God not providing for me the desires of my heart? As I waited for answers to these questions, I learned how to understand Jeremiah 29 more deeply and, more importantly, how to recognize the subtle ways that my view of God plans being twisted to make myself feel comfortable.

My life is nothing like I planned, but when I look back, I'm grateful. I can't imagine how hectic and crazy my life would be if God had given me all of my desires on my time. I wanted to be married by 25, with an amazing job, a two story home and I wanted to live in California. Let me be honest, If I had married the man I was with at 25, I would probably be divorced, bankrupt and miserable. God ALWAYS knows what's best. He also knows that you're capable of more than you think. Your penthouse thought is God's basement idea.

I remember walking into my local grocery store and an older guy asked if I wanted to sign up to take pictures. I told him no, because the date of the pictures was the day of a speaking engagement that I was booked for. He let out the most annoying laugh, looked at me sideways and said, "With a voice like that…who would listen to you?" I smirked and walked away, but deep down my feelings were hurt. I've had the same reaction countless times when people have heard me speak and every time, I would laugh it off, but then I realized sometimes God allows you to go through the same test and over and over until you pass it. I could have easily passed the test by explaining how blessed I am to even be alive, encouraging others faith in God or even testifying on the goodness of Jesus, but before that day I had never taken the opportunity to do so. It's funny that medical doctors said I would never speak, but God has allowed me to speak in front of huge crowds, reaching thousands of people. It's amazing that God will use the most humiliating parts of your life and allow you it to be a testament of his grace and mercy.

Scripture Reading:

Jeremiah 29:11

"For I know the plans I have for you," declares the Lord, "plans to prosper you and not to harm you, plans to give you hope and a future."

Devotional Reading:

Does this ever happen to you…you get in the car with a group of friends or your family and ask: "Where do you want to eat?" "I don't care. Where do you want to eat?" "It doesn't matter to me, what are you in the mood for?" "Anything is fine with me. Whatever you want will be great." And it goes round and round until finally someone says: "Just pick somewhere already. I'm hungry." If we have that much trouble choosing a place to go eat, how are we ever going to pick a path for our lives? How are we ever going to choose the more important issues of career, spouse, higher education, city to live in, and the thousand other decisions that face us on our journey of life? The exciting news is we don't have to figure all that out. We just have to listen to the One who has figured all that out and do what He tells us to do. God has a plan for you and your life.

Jeremiah 29:11 begins by stating the fact that God has a plan for you. God knows what He wants you to do. He knows where He wants you to live. He knows what job He wants you to have. He knows who He wants you to marry. God has a path spelled out for your life. He knows the plans He has for you.

And even more exciting is that God makes good plans. God actually knows what He is doing when He spells out His plans for you. His plans are plans that will "prosper you" and "not harm you." His plans will lead to the best possible life you can have. God wants to bless you and show His favor in your life. He makes good plans.

Finally, God's plans give you hope and a great future. Here is the truth about how God lays out His plans: When you get to the end of your life, looking back at all that will have occurred over your years on earth, you would have chosen God's plan for you every time because from that perspective you can see every great result that comes from following His will. Looking from there, we would choose it because we can see where it ends up. From where we are today, we must choose that path in faith. But, it is still a great, hope-filled, prosperous plan that is the best route to choose in our lives.

Have you ever trusted your Navigation App in such a way that you have no idea where you are, you are just trusting the voice in your phone to lead you to where you want to be? Turn here. Turn there. Go this way. You took a route you would have never chosen to take but you ended up right where you wanted to be. God works that way. Trust Him with the turns in life and you will end up right where you want to be. He does know what He is doing. Will you follow His plan for your life? When it is all said and done, you'll be glad you did.

Devotional Questions

1. Reflect on a time when you made plans and they didn't go through. Reflect on how God turned your disappointment into something great for your life.

_____

_____

_____

_____

_____

_____

_____

_____

_____

_____

_____

_____

_____

_____

_____

2. What role does God have in your plans?

_____

_____

_____

_____

_____

_____

_____

_____

_____

_____

_____

_____

_____

_____

3. What have you learned about God's plans for your life based on this past year?

_____

_____

_____

_____

_____

_____

_____

_____

_____

_____

4. How would you describe the hope and faith that you have in Jesus Christ?

_____

_____

_____

_____

_____

_____

_____

_____

_____

_____

_____

_____

_____

Today is: _____

Memory Verse or Inspirational Scripture:	Prayer and Thanksgiving for Myself:
My Confessions:	Prayers for Others:

Day FIVE

Love

Puppy Love.

My first real boyfriend was so cool. I was in the 9th grade when I met the love of my life (at the time). I had no idea what love was, but he was popular, tall, dark and handsome. We "dated" for a while, then one day out of the blue, he broke up with me in front of everyone. I was devastated. I ran to the bathroom and cried. When I came out, he was with another girl and he seemed so happy. In my mind, I was the girl who was always rejected, never good enough to be seen as pretty and I felt so ugly at that point. Not only outside, but inside too.

My best friend, at the time decided it was time for me to come out of my slump and find someone new. She ended up calling me on three- way and introducing me to a guy from our rival school. The guy and I hit it off and the rest was history; or so I thought.

I've dealt with physical and verbal abuse from people who said they loved me. I accepted less than I deserved, because I did not love myself enough to realize that just because someone couldn't see what God saw in me, that didn't mean I wasn't special. At the time, I had no idea what it truly meant to love someone. I remember when I was younger, I would watch movies, the news or hear about abuse victims, but I never believed it would be me. The first time I was ever hit, I blamed myself for it. I was in the living room with my new boyfriend. I confronted him about being with another girl and he slapped me. From then on, anytime he disliked something I said, got angry or simply felt like it, he would hit me. I never told anyone. I was embarrassed and I didn't understand how someone who loved me could hurt me.

God sent me several signs to let me know this person wasn't the one. The abuse initially started with words of belittlement. His friends would call me ugly, he would laugh and agree. He would tell me nobody else would ever want me if I left him, so I may as well accept the treatment. Nothing I ever did was good enough for him. And I started to equate love to sex. I felt that if he wanted to have sex with me, then that made me pretty. Sex was love to me; even if I didn't want to do it.

There were times I was forced to have sex with him. He would hit me, call me names, drag me up and down my drive way, only to take me back in the house and force himself on me. I knew that if I told someone, I would then have to confess to all the days I skipped school for him and all of the times I let him inside my mother's house without her permission for the umpteenth time. I felt trapped. I felt my only way out was death. I desperately wanted to end the nightmare I was going through.

After giving birth to two of his children, I felt that maybe God wanted me here. Maybe God wanted me to stay with this man. Why else would he allow me to get pregnant...AGAIN? I was on birth control...so how in the world did this happen? So many other people were ding way more than I was...so why didn't this happen to them? I decided to write him a letter, asking him to stop, but he never received the letter, because my mother found it. Needless to say, she was enraged. She banned him from her house and told me to leave him alone.

Thank God, I finally woke up and listened. My mother started to force me to listen to "Me" By Tamia. To this day, I know the song word for word and I even have let my daughter listen to the song. The words resonate with me in my adulthood. The song describes a woman who has finally decided to love herself before anyone else. I decided to go off to college and build a better future for my children. I never looked back. I finally learned the true meaning of love in a loveless world.

Love in a Loveless World

Scripture Reading:

1 Corinthians 13:4 (NIV)

Love is patient, love is kind. It does not envy, it does not boast, it is not proud.

Devotional Reading:

We live in a messed up world. Ceaseless wars rage because nations cannot get along. Too many innocent people are affected by senseless crime. Scientists argue about how the earth is or is not impacted our industrialized lifestyle and what should be done about it. Most pursue those things that are best for "me" while giving little to no thought of how to help or even give a second thought to others. Indeed, we live in a messed up world.

One area of life that the world just cannot understand is the area of love. Most will assume that means the romantic kind of dating love. But, true love goes much, much deeper than that. True love is that which is experienced in families between parents and children, brothers and sisters. True love is lived out between lifelong friends who have walked through the fires together. True love is the husband sitting by the bedside of his wife of 50 plus years while she labors to breathe because of cancer. True love is the co-workers who stay late to help out the new employee get the project done. True love looks out for others and is willing to give of ourselves. The world has great difficulty in understanding that kind of love and living that kind of love.

In 1 Corinthians 13, Paul gives a beautiful explanation of what true love looks like. He begins by stating: "Love is patient." Love hangs in there even when the other person doesn't deserve to be loved. Love gives room for grace. Love doesn't expect perfection and doesn't give up when perfection is not achieved. Love is patient.

Paul also says that "love is kind." Love shows compassion. Love seeks to bless and encourage rather than point out every shortcoming in others. Love seeks for the best for others. Love is kind.

Then, Paul transitions from the outward display of patience and kindness to the inward reality that love "does not envy, it does not boast, it is not proud." Envy says, "I deserve this rather than you." Love says, "Let me celebrate the way God has blessed you." Boasting and pride point out how awesome I am. Love pursues the enrichment of others, even if no one notices me at all. True love thinks about others.

Through the rest of 1 Corinthians 13, Paul lists several characteristics of what true love looks like and how it is lived out. This love is a selfless, sacrificial, God-like kind of love. The best example of that love is the love that God showed for us by sending His One and Only Son, Jesus, to die on the cross for our sins. That is the epitome of a selfless, sacrificial, God-like love. And that is the way God has called us to love each other.

The world does not love like that. But God does. And we should too. Let's learn how to love from our heavenly Father, not from the world around us. True love is loving like God loves.

Devotional Questions

1. According to 1 John 4:9, how does God show his love?

    _____

    _____

_____

_____

_____

_____

_____

_____

_____

2. If a person says that they are a Christian, but shows their lack of love through bitterness, anger and an unforgiving spirit, should we affirm that he is a Christian? Why or why not?

_____

_____

_____

_____

_____

_____

_____

3. What is the definition of AGAPE LOVE to you?

_____

_____

_____

Today is:_____

Memory Verse or Inspirational Scripture:	Prayer and Thanksgiving for Myself:
My Confessions:	Prayers for Others:

Day SIX

Being an Esther Woman

Maybe if I pray enough it will go away. 200 sit ups a day will keep the tummy away. My mom is going to kill me if she finds out I'm pregnant AGAIN. I seriously thought the Depo shot worked. Sitting in the doctor's office of an abortion clinic, I was scared out of my mind. Hearing the shuffling of feet going back and forth, looking at other women and wondering what they were here for. "She's going straight to school after this abortion. I'm so sick of this", screamed one girl's mother. I sat there looking terrified.

Why am I even here? I know I don't need another baby, but I don't want to kill this one either. Maybe I can put him up for adoption. Everything around me pointed to abortion. "Get rid of it and move on with your life." "You have so much future ahead of you…there is no way you are ever going to be able to do it with two kids." Those words resonated with me and played over and over again in my head. I'm only 17…People are going to call me a slut and they are going to laugh at me. My mind was everywhere. But the truth was…I was 17 and in a relationship and I thought I was in love. I was too busy focusing on and looking for something I was never even missing, that I didn't even notice that the love I was looking for was already instilled inside of me. I had already had a baby at 16, but that wasn't planned. I was on birth control and now I'm pregnant again. I've never been "fast", I don't party and drink, so why me? I always knew not to question God, but who else could answer my questions? God why have you forsaken me? I'm nothing like those girls that get pregnant as teenagers.

Walking down the hall, I opened the door to the abortion clinic. I was scared, but I was ready to get things over with. I knew I didn't want another child and I felt this was the biggest mistake of my life. I could handle one, but I couldn't handle the humiliation of being a teen mom of two. My family's reputation was on the line. I had to do something. My mom signed the papers and asked if this was what I wanted to do... I said yes. The wait was taking forever. "Once you get rid of this baby you're going straight to school", screamed one girls' mom. I was so nervous. In my heart, I knew this wasn't the right thing to do, but at the same time I felt in order to be successful in life I needed to do this. I didn't care about Gods approval or about him forgiving me at the time.

It is the Lord who goes before you. He will be with you; he will not leave you or forsake you. Do not fear or be dismayed." -Deuteronomy 31:8

We tend to blame God for our consequences after being disobedient. I knew better. I LIVED in church. I was an usher, I was in the choir, I even taught bible study some days....so how could THIS be happening to ME? After waiting about 30 minutes, I was called to the back for an ultrasound. Afterwards, they let me watch a video of the abortion process and then the doctor looked at me and said..." Maybe you should come back tomorrow...think it over and make sure you want to really do this..." You can't imagine how relieved I was. I was scared to get an abortion. I was scared that I would regret it. I was scared to go through with the entire process and most of all...even in my mess, I was afraid of letting God down.

The most important thing she'd learned over the years was that there was no way to be a perfect mother and a million

ways to be a good one.
– Jill Churchill

5 months later, I went into labor.

My entire world came crashing down all at once. Here I am….17 and a mother of two beautiful children. I knew nothing about kids. I was an only child all my life. I didn't even understand how to get along with people who lived with me, so how on earth would I ever be good enough to be someone's mother. I felt helpless. I felt like a failure and because of this, I fell into a deep depression. Something that would carry on for the next 8 years of my life.

My mother tried to get me to see that everything I was searching for in other people, I never needed. I didn't want to listen. I was too busy trying to fit in and be cool. Deep inside I was hurting and longing for the acceptance of my peers, but while I was doing that, I completely lost myself. I never took the time to truly understand myself as a person. I had no idea who I was, who I belonged to, what God had in store for me or anything. I knew nothing about what God thought of me, even though I attended church and was extremely active, I just didn't get it.

I remember being so desperate for a way out that I went into my closet and put a belt around my neck. I was too afraid to hang myself, so I took a few pills and ended up spending a week in a mental health facility. When I got there, I knew I didn't belong there, but like always...I couldn't figure out exactly where I belonged. It's amazing how God keeps us even in the midst of our recklessness. My most embarrassing moment ended up completely turning my life around for the better. Today, my son is 10 years old and my daughter id 12 and they are the highlight of my life. I can't imagine my life without them. God knew exactly what I needed to make me start to turn my life around. I am so glad, God set my mistakes up to turn into to messages of hope. God is faithful. He makes no mistakes.

I wanted to change my life. I wanted to give God the glory and I wanted to allow him to use me no matter what my past looked like. The story of Esther is an amazing example of a woman who fully trusts God. Esther was a dynamic woman. She did the right thing no matter what could have possibly happen. As women, we should strive to have the characteristics of Esther.

Scripture Reading

Esther 4:14, 16

(Mordecai's answer): *"And who knows but that you have come to your royal position for such a time as this?"*

(Esther replied): *"And if I perish, I perish."*

Devotional Reading:

The *Miss America Pageant*, the *Miss USA Pageant*, and the *Miss Universe Pageant* are all attempts to crown a young lady that possesses striking beauty and a winsome personality. These are the big ones. All across the country from city festivals to county fairs, young ladies are crowned anything from Miss Snake Charmer in Sweetwater, Texas to Miss Catfish in Belzoni, Mississippi. (Amazingly, these are actual pageants.) But, all pageants have one major flaw. The judges are only able to look at the outside and possibly analyze some short answers to questions or see a talent of some sort, but no human judge can look at the inside of any of the young ladies. But, God can.

One major truth that we learn from Esther is that she possesses both an outer beauty and an inner beauty. The outer beauty is seen in the way that she becomes the favorite of King Xerxes. He was looking for the most beautiful women in his land, and Esther was one of those selected. Then, Esther rose to be the favorite of King Xerxes (see Esther 2:17). No doubt that it was Esther striking beauty that initially won her the favor of the king. There is nothing wrong with being beautiful on the outside as long as we understand that this beauty is from the Lord, this beauty can be used for the Lord's glory rather than for our personal gain, and outward beauty will never replace inward beauty. Esther had this outer beauty and served God with this outer beauty.

Much of this outer beauty is determined by how God wove our DNA for us to look like we look. Much of the inner beauty is determined by how we let the Spirit of God grow us to be women who seek God, walk with God, and serve God. Esther had this inner beauty, too. When faced with the opportunity to help her people, the Israelites, Esther rose to the challenge, even though it put her life in great danger. In fact, Mordecai (Esther's uncle) challenged Esther by letting her know that it might even be for this very moment of acting on behalf of the Israelites that God placed her in the very position where she finds herself.

When faced with this dilemma of risking her own life in order to stand up on behalf of her people. Esther responded with the faith that stated she would leave it all in God's hands. "If I perish, I perish," she concluded. That is inner beauty. That is inner strength. That is a woman who is serving God with everything that she has and trusting Him with the results.

When faced with choosing between outer beauty and inner beauty, Esther taught us that outer beauty is fine and might can even be used by the Lord, but inner beauty is preferable. There is nothing more beautiful than a Christian lady living for the Lord in a way that honors and serves Him. That is what God is looking for. And, He is more important than any pageant judge could ever be.

Devotional Questions:

1. Where do you see God's hand moving in circumstances in your life right now?

   _____

   _____

   _____

   _____

   _____

   _____

   _____

2. Think of a time in which God has placed you to do his will. What risks do you face in doing the right thing?

_____

_____

_____

_____

_____

_____

_____

_____

3. What character qualities must you exhibit in order to do the right thing?

_____

_____

_____

_____

_____

_____

_____

_____

Today is:_____

Memory Verse or Inspirational Scripture:	Prayer and Thanksgiving for Myself:
My Confessions:	Prayers for Others:

Day SEVEN

Broken Hearts

I never really learned to love myself until a few years ago when I had to make a huge decision about who I would spend the rest of my life with. For so long, I wanted to make everything look as if it was perfect and fine. I lived up to everybody else's expectations... especially in my love life. I wanted to date someone older, someone "cool", someone different. I felt like I needed to stay with someone because everyone else thought that we were the perfect match, but after years of putting up with NOT being loved. I finally realized this wasn't what I really wanted or needed. Now let's be clear. No relationship is perfect, but the fact of the matter is... God will send you signs. It's up to us to take them for what they are. I ignored them. The lies, pregnancy scares from other women, the cheating... our "love" was something straight out of a mystery book of love scandals... One of those novels you just can't quite seem to put down. And I was the leading actress. dressed in my pretty clothes and heels, carrying my huge purses, hiding my tears behind shades, so that nobody else could see.

I thought that the rings he gave me meant something. The promises... I believed those too. Or maybe I was fooling myself. Hoping so hard to find the love that God had for me in a man. It almost always starts beautifully, but the ending is the most interesting part. My senior year of college was supposed to be the best year of my life, right? The bridge to adulthood, but not quite... those moments where you're still free enough to be wild and act immature, but mature enough to get things done and set a future for yourself. My grades were perfect and I participated in so many events, including the Homecoming Parade. I was in so many activities from fashion shows to student activity clubs. Even in the middle of depression, I easily put on a front. I would smile, walk out of my dorm and pretend to be the happiest girl in the world, when in reality I was so lonely.

There were times when we fought...with words and hands...in front of people. They would laugh and talk, not understanding why so many emotions were flying through me. I was angry. Angry because the person I loved was a liar. The person I fell in love with was making a fool of me and I knew it. I was too weak to leave and too afraid to start over alone or with someone else. After all, 4 years is so much to invest for me to be so young. When graduation rolled around, I didn't cry at all. I felt so many emotions. Sadness wasn't one of them. I was content, because I was leaving. As I left the campus, I felt weights lifted off of my shoulders.

But once again, we made it work, but then I found out about another woman and my heart just couldn't let me be okay with this. I couldn't look at him without thinking about what he had done with these other women. I was falling out of love and I was unhappy. I stopped calling. I stopped showing affection. I stopped everything and finally … I left. I just couldn't spend the rest of my life with a man who I felt didn't love me. I knew that my breaking point was coming. I knew that it was only a matter of time and I'm so happy and I feel so free, because I don't have to worry about being hurt anymore.

And even though I've been through all of that and then some. . I still believe in the power of love, because God is love. I still have so much love in my heart to give. So to everyone in my past thank you. It doesn't take long to know when you've met your soulmate and fallen in love with God and yourself. But it's sad that it took me so long to realize that I hadn't met my soul in any of the people, places and things that I attempted to find contentment in.

With all of this being said, I feel empowered. I don't care how long you've been with someone. . if they aren't treating you right, then leave. Love isn't always enough to stay in a bad situation. Holding on to the wrong person, could keep you from getting the blessing that God has waiting for you. I'm content with the fact that I finally opened my eyes and my heart and was strong enough to let go and I thank God for holding my hand through my mess of mistakes.

I was never really ready for a relationship in the first place, because I had yet to heal from my past. I was devastated and it led me to seek comfort in drinking and clubbing. I never really felt comfortable in clubs, but I felt I needed to do something to pass the time. I was so depressed that I would drink so much, I no longer got drunk. My body literally seemed to become immune to alcohol. I would go to class, go back to my room and drink. Between classes, I would drink, but I somehow managed to hold everything together for the public. I would go through my week, smiling and doing anything most normal college students did, but on the weekends, I would lock my door, lay in the middle of my floor and cry from Friday night until Sunday.

On Sunday's something (the Holy Spirit), would lead me to get up, dry my tears and go to church. I was so depressed, that I barely would eat. My clothes were starting to get too big for me and at the time I was only about 100 pounds, soaking wet. Nobody kept me from losing my mind during this time, except Jesus. I desperately needed Him. I would force myself to go to every revival and church service on campus. I needed less of me and more of God. I didn't see a future for myself. I didn't even see past the end of the day.

One evening during revival, a prophetess called me by name. When she called my name, I looked around, wondering who else in the building had my name. She called my name again and told me to stop looking around. She told me I would lose my boyfriend, most of my friends, and I was called to do something bigger than myself. The prophetess began to tell me how I would speak to thousands of people and that God has amazing plans for my life, but I would have to go through many trials to see the fruit of it all. I didn't believe a word she said. How in the world could God love a woman like me? With so much loss and heartbreak in my life, how could God ever use me? And there was no way I would be caught speaking to anyone, much less thousands of people. I felt like I was a little TOO broken to be used by the Lord, but needless to say, she was right about everything.

Scripture Reading:

Psalm 34:18

The Lord is close to the brokenhearted and saves those who are crushed in spirit.

Devotional Reading:

Isn't it so irritating when we see people who seem to have everything in their life together? They do not have a hair out of place. They never seem to lose their temper or say embarrassing comments. They never seem frustrated or overwhelmed or at a loss for words. Everything seems to be going perfect…all the time.

Those people are so irritating to us because we know that our lives our not like that. In fact, for many, our lives are the total opposite of that. We are rushing out the door to face the day not able to take the time to be sure we are all "put together." We have trouble eating because we tend to always stick our foot in our mouth. We are frustrated at the way things pile up in our lives and overwhelmed with our to-do list that only seems to have things added and never seems to have anything marked off.

We readily admit that we are less than perfect…all the time.

God has a word for those of us who carry more consistently the title of "Imperfect" rather than "Perfect." In Psalm 34:18, we see that God stays close to "the brokenhearted." The Lord realizes that we are less than perfect and that life is piling up on us. He knows the issues and events in our lives that have broken our hearts. He sees how deep our hurt is and how weak and insignificant we feel. He understands the circumstances that surround us that weigh incredibly heavy on our souls and make it hard to roll out of bed each day. God sees. He knows. He cares. And, He stays close. "The Lord is close to the brokenhearted."

Has your heart been broken? Have the circumstances around you made it feel like your life is crashing in around you? Take heart, friend. The Lord is still close to you. He draws near at our point of biggest need. His love has not wavered. His presence has not gone AWOL. His connection to us is not shattered. He hasn't gone anywhere. He is close.

Maybe in your life, the term "brokenhearted" is an understatement. Maybe you feel totally demolished by what life has thrown your way. Maybe you feel defeated and abandoned. Maybe you have lost all hope. Maybe life is just too much right now. Hear this promise about what the Lord does: He "saves those who are crushed in spirit." He rescues those who are past the end of their rope. He liberates those who are being held hostage by the circumstances they face.

If you describe yourself as "brokenhearted" or "crushed in spirit," then God's word has great news for you. You have not been forgotten. In fact, you are far from forgotten. God promises that He is close to you. And, He promises that He will save you from the craziness, the lostness, the hopelessness, and the helplessness that you feel. His love will not let you go. Not now. Not ever.

Devotional Questions

1. What does Psalm 34:18 mean to you?

   _____

   _____

   _____

   _____

   _____

   _____

_____

_____

_____

_____

_____

2. *Fear of the Lord* is an older term for "respect and submission to God." We should be afraid of offending God with conscious acts of disobedience. We should fear the wrath of God because of our disobedience. What temptations are you facing now?

_____

_____

_____

_____

_____

_____

_____

_____

_____

_____

_____

_____

_____

_____

_____

3. How can learning the fear of the Lord keep you
   acting and thinking righteously?

   _____

   _____

   _____

   _____

   _____

   _____

   _____

   _____

   _____

Today is: _____

Memory Verse or Inspirational Scripture:	Prayer and Thanksgiving for Myself:
My Confessions:	Prayers for Others:

Day EIGHT

Sexual Purity

Many people say the definition of insanity is doing the same things over and over and expecting different results. The true definition of insanity is knowing exactly what God has commanded you to do (or not do) and still doing it anyway.

Today, it seems that sex is everywhere. The less clothes you have on, the more people flock to you. The more sexual you portray yourself to be, the more "popular" you become. I went through a phase where I equated sex to love. I felt that if someone wanted to have sex with me, then they loved me. I would give myself away to people and I felt like it was okay, because I "knew" them or "we were friends first". Nothing I was doing honored God in any way and I knew it. After a short, worthless session of fornication, I almost always felt convicted. I would lie to myself and make myself believe that if I went to church on Sundays and went to bible studies on Wednesdays, then a little sex every now and then really didn't matter. God would still forgive me, but that was the furthest things from the truth. I was filthy on the inside. My heart wasn't pure, so my "worship" on Sundays meant nothing, because I was back to being wordly as soon as I stepped out of church.

Everything around me was falling apart. I kept wondering why God wasn't answering any of my prayers. Psalms 34:17 clearly states that God hears the prayers of the righteous. (The righteous cry out, and the LORD hears them; he delivers them from all their troubles.) God began to strip everything away from me. My eyes began to open and I realized I was creating soul ties with people who weren't even meant to be apart of my life. I started to fast and pray and ask God for a release. I asked Him to take any sexual desires away from me until marriage. I began to get so desperate for God that anyone who stood in my way had an open door to leave. Nothing else mattered to me anymore, except my relationship with the Lord.

I was tired of only seeking God because I was desperate and waiting for a husband that was never promised to me. I wanted more of Jesus. I wanted to know everything about him! I wanted the honeymoon stage with the Lord to last forever and I wanted to learn to love Him in spite of. The same way he loved me unconditionally. Would I truly be satisfied if I was called into a life of singleness? Would I be able to be apart of fulfilling his mission to gain souls for Christ, even if he never did anything else for me? Was I as desperate for God, like I was as desperate for a man? The love I was searching for was here all along.

I took a personal vow of celibacy. I did not decide to become celibate, so that God could send me a husband. I didn't have a hidden motive for God to grant me all of my desires. I was celibate, because I wanted to obey God. I told the Lord that even if I was called into a life of singleness, that I would honor him with my heart, mind and body. Sex left me empty and convicted, with a void no human on earth could fulfill. Imagine loving someone with all of your heart and soul and every day, they ripped your heart out, knowing the things they were doing were unpleasing to you. That's exactly how we make God feel with we blatantly do the things that he has told us not to do. Temporary pleasure will never lead to permanent satisfaction.

Scripture Reading:

1 Thessalonians 4:3-4 (NIV)

It is God's will that you should be sanctified: that you should avoid sexual immorality; that each of you should learn to control your own body in a way that is holy and honorable.

Devotional Reading:

Sexual expression is everywhere: movies, music, videos, conversations, Facebook, Instagram…everywhere. Our culture is selling sex, promoting sex, and proclaiming that sexual activity is the norm. Those who are following Christ are being bombarded with the lie that being sexually active will satisfy the deep need for intimacy. We cannot look to society to learn what God's call in the area of sexuality is.

Instead, as Christians should in every area of our lives, we must look to Scripture to learn what God expects from us and how God protects us in this area of sex. 1 Thessalonians 4 is very clear that God's will for His children is that we should avoid sexual immorality. That simply means that God wants us to save our sexual activity to share with our husband or wife in the bounds of a God-ordained marriage. How can believers in Christ win the battle of staying sexually pure in such a sexually charged society? Here are three keys to winning that battle.

1. *Recognize the Standard*

God has set certain standards for our protection and for our good. God's call to holiness is not arbitrary and confining. God is not trying to ruin our fun or be the cosmic killjoy. God knows what is best for us. And, God has said that what is in our best interest for our relationship with Him and with others, including our boyfriend or girlfriend, is to wait until after marriage to express the sexual component of our relationship. It is for our good that God set this standard.

2. *Understand the Cost*

Choosing to be sexually active does bring a great cost to the individual and the relationship. We carry every sexual partner we ever have for the rest of our lives. Do we really want to bring several or many people, or even just one other person, into our marriage bedroom when we find that person that God sends our way to spend the rest of our lives with who we have fallen madly in love with? It will cost us baggage and tension in the most important human relationship we will have, our marriage. This does not even consider the very real possibility of an unwanted pregnancy or sexually transmitted diseases. God knows that it costs us something to be sexually active before marriage, and that cost is simply too high.

3. Relish the Reward

One day, after a beautiful wedding, you will close the bedroom door and have the opportunity to share the most physically intimate act with the person that you will love most in this world, your new spouse. You have a special gift that you can only give to one person, your purity. Wouldn't you like to be able to give to that most special person on that most special night that most special gift? If you carelessly throw that gift away and waste it on someone else, you will not have that gift to give.

God knows what He's doing when He calls us to wait until we are married to be sexually active. Let's listen to that call and live up to that standard. We will be glad we did.

Devotional Questions

1. If you're practicing celibacy, what are your reasons? Are you seeking God more for a husband or for your salvation?

_____

_____

_____

_____

_____

_____

_____

_____

_____

_____

_____

2. What are soul ties? How can they be broken?

_____

_____

_____

_____

_____

_____

_____

_____

_____

Today is: _____

Memory Verse or Inspirational Scripture:	Prayer and Thanksgiving for Myself:
My Confessions:	Prayers for Others:

Day NINE

Grace

Before becoming a teen mother, I was the typical "church girl". I went to every meeting at church, from prayer meetings to bible study to morning and evening services. I loved the Lord, but I didn't have a clear understanding of all I had been through before my pregnancy. I took life for granted and because being sick was "normal" for me, I never realized how blessed I was to be given life.

God's grace has followed me all of my life. When I was 9 years old, the walls of my throat collapsed. I was rushed to surgery and I ended up having a bone graph. A bone was taken from my rib and put into my throat. 19 years later, the bone is still holding the walls of my throat open. I was supposed to e in a coma for weeks during and after the surgery. None of that happened and it's only by his grace that I'm still able to tell the story of my life.

I ran from God for so long. I rejected his love for me, thinking that I could live however I wanted, because I was young. People are dying every day, but I didn't think about my days being numbered by God. I just wanted to live. I felt that I had already done and been through so many horrible things, that God didn't need me to obey him, but I was wrong.

God will lead us to the path, he will equip us with the directions, he'll so kindly program the GPS within us, but it's up to us to walk the path he has set for us. I spent so many years, contemplating writing this book. God sent so many people my way to confirm what he already told me was within me. I sat and doubted myself. I allowed the words of others to make me feel less than. "She doesn't even know who she is in Christ". "She doesn't even know anything about the bible." "Her personality is just too much." For a while, I believed the seeds the enemy planted about me. But then I realized, sitting back and lingering on the opinions of people who never took the time to get to know me would only hinder my growth. I know that my big personality, my wisdom from experience and my personal relationship with God was something someone needed to hear. It was needed and I knew this, because everything I've been through was all apart of Gods purpose and plan for my life.

The enemy will always try to destroy you, because he knows what God has in store for you. The enemy knows that God can and will use your life to bring others to Christ if you obey the call of the Lord. Your battles belong to the Lord.

Scripture Reading:

1 Peter 5:10 (NIV)

And the God of all grace, who called you to his eternal glory in Christ, after you have suffered a little while, will himself restore you and make you strong, firm and steadfast.

Devotional Reading:

"Grace" is definitely a God-word. We would know nothing about grace without God's example of what grace looks like. And, grace from God comes in several different forms. Grace is received by everyone as the sun comes up every morning. That is God's general grace to all. Grace is received by Christians as God washes us clean from sin. That is God's forgiving grace. Grace comes in big doses to those who are suffering for the name of Jesus. That is God's sustaining grace. This is the grace we see in 1 Peter 5:10.

Some struggle mightily with the concept that Christians suffer in this life. Whether that suffering comes because of circumstances in life or because of a believer taking a stand for the cause of Christ, the fact that a Christian would suffer at all can be puzzling. Wouldn't it be right for the "good" among us who claim the name of Christ to not suffer? Shouldn't the suffering be saved for the "bad" among us who deserve it? That is our thinking. Often, that is not God's thinking.

God knows something that we don't always realize: a special presence of God and a special grace from God accompanies the suffering that comes when we stand for Christ. We experience the Lord in ways we will never experience apart from suffering. Many followers of Jesus have ended up thanking God for the times of suffering because of the unmistakable presence of God and grace of God that they received.

This grace is a precious, wonderful thing. The above verse points out a couple of important truths. First, the suffering is only short term. "After you have suffered a little while..." lets us know that the suffering will end. It is limited in length and in scope. God's grace mandates that. Second, God, through grace, will restore His child. When all is said and done, God's grace ensures that the Christian will be better off than before the suffering. Everything will be returned or improved. The result of suffering will never cost anything that is not restored. Finally, God will strengthen the one suffering making her stand longer and truer in Christ.

The epitome of grace is that God uses even the times of struggle and pain to work out perseverance and even victory in the life of the sufferer. One reason this is so beautiful is because this is actually occurring all over the world and has throughout the history of the church. In the verse before our verse, Peter writes "…because you know that the family of believers throughout the world is undergoing the same kind of sufferings" (1 Peter 5:9, NIV). Many in Christ face tough times because of Christ. But, God's grace sustains…always.

Are you suffering through life? Are you suffering for Christ? Take heart, you are not alone. Others suffer too. God knows. God sees. God cares. God is the God of all grace and will pour out His grace on you.

Devotional Questions

1. How can God's glory be a means of grace to renounce the manifestations of your sin?

   _____

   _____

   _____

_____

_____

_____

_____

_____

_____

2. What amazes you about God's Grace?

_____

_____

_____

_____

_____

_____

_____

3. As a Christian, do you expect God to save you from suffering or do you expect to suffer for Christ in the midst of a world that does not operate according to His will?

_____

_____

_____

_____

_____

_____

_____

_____

_____

_____

_____

_____

4. Read Philippians 3:10. What is Paul's perspective on suffering?

_____

_____

_____

_____

_____

_____

_____

_____

_____

_____

Today is: _____

Memory Verse or Inspirational Scripture:	Prayer and Thanksgiving for Myself:
My Confessions:	Prayers for Others:

Day TEN

Mercy

Mercy: God's Love Through Patience

Because of my previous surgeries, I was scheduled to go to my Otolaryngoligist once a year. I had been in remission since I was 9 years old and I figured I was in the clear. I skipped my appointment in 2012, because I was busy. Time went on and I started to feel terrible. I was working an awesome job at a hospital back in 2013. I absolutely love my patients and I was always eager to go to work. During this time, I began to lose weight. I noticed that I was always tired. It was getting harder and harder to me to catch my breath and doing simple tasks at work seemed to take the life and energy out of me. I quickly scheduled an appointment with my doctor. I felt like I was about 99% sure that it would be like any other appointment. I figured I would go into the office, he would put the scope up my nose and down my throat and he would say nothing was there and I would move on with my life.

This time was different. As he put the scope down my throat, he paused for a second, which seemed like an eternity. He said, "I see a growth on your vocal cords…you're going to need surgery immediately". I was devastated. I had plans to be in a wedding and to go to the Bahamas the following week. Even in the middle of something that could change my life, I was more concerned with "living", not realizing my life was possibly on the line.

I left the office in tears and went home to prepare for my surgery the following Tuesday. When I told my mom, she began to tear up, which made me feel even worse. I didn't understand why after all this time in remission, I had to go through this for the hundredth time. I just wanted to go back to my normal life. I wanted to go back to work and just live, but this wasn't the case.

Tuesday morning came and I checked in for surgery. This was something I was used to doing, but I was still nervous. So many thoughts ran through my head as I was led to my hospital room. The doctors and nurses came in to tell me to go ahead and change clothes, remove any piercings I had and prepare to be taken down for the surgery. I did as I was instructed and the nurses eventually came in to take me into the surgery.

During and after this experience, I learned that life should never be taken for granted. Our health is not promised to us and it's so easy to think you'll never be in a situation, but God is the author of our life. We should always be grateful for each day God has allowed us to live. I was arrogant in the way that I took my health for granted. Not realizing that remission doesn't mean you're completely cured. Sometimes God will put us into a position where we are forced to lean on him and the only thing that can save us is His Grace and Mercy.

Scripture Reading:

Titus 3:4-6 (NIV)

[4] But when the kindness and love of God our Savior appeared, [5] he saved us, not because of righteous things we had done, but because of his mercy. He saved us through the washing of rebirth and renewal by the Holy Spirit, [6] whom he poured out on us generously through Jesus Christ our Savior.

Devotional Reading:

We hear about God's grace often. And we should. If God's grace is God giving us what we don't deserve, then God's mercy is God NOT giving us what we do deserve. We do not have to read much of the Bible to understand that we deserve God's judgment, His wrath, His anger, His discipline, His punishment, and all around "Zap" from God. But, that is not who God is. That is not His character.

Rather than giving us what we deserve, God loves to show us mercy. That is the very nature of who He is as a loving God.

Now don't misunderstand, God is a holy God and a just God. He can and will pour out His wrath to everyone who refuses to turn to Him. But, to those who by faith will respond to His love offered through what Jesus did on the cross, God will gladly pour out His mercy. Notice these four things about God's mercy:

1. God saves us through His mercy. Our very salvation comes because God is willing to show His great mercy to those who call out to Him.

2. We cannot earn His mercy. It is not because of the "righteous things we had done" but solely because of His mercy. We have not earned it. We cannot earn it. He chooses to give it.

3. His mercy is an internal work in us. "He saved us through the washing of rebirth." This washing is a washing away of our sin because of His mercy. And, it brings a "rebirth," a new start, another

chance. He shows the mercy of giving us another try in Christ.

4. His mercy is highlighted by His Spirit doing a work of remaking us from the inside out. The Holy Spirit is God's mercy personified. He comes to live in us. He comes to clean us up. He comes to strengthen us. He comes to guide us. He is the merciful God in us.

5. His mercy is given generously through Jesus Christ. God does not use an eyedropper to dole out His mercy. He uses a fire hose. His mercy is constant. And, His mercy is huge. His mercy is consistent, and His mercy is overwhelming.

Ultimately, God's mercy shows His love and builds on His grace. But, His mercy is that in

God which withholds what we deserve so that He can give us what we don't deserve. How can you quantify that which is immeasurable? How can you fully describe that which is beyond comprehension? The answer is "you can't." So, rather than trying to define God's mercy, let's savor in it. Rather than trying to grasp it, let's fall headlong into His mercy. There will be no softer place to land than in the arms of a merciful God. Thank you, Lord, for Your mercy.

Devotional Questions

1. Mercy is one of God's most highlighted characteristics. Why do you think the bible emphasizes so much on God's mercy?

_____

_____

_____

_____

_____

_____

_____

_____

_____

2. Study and Find an example in scripture where God shows mercy to someone in the bible.

_____

_____

_____

_____

_____

_____

_____

_____

_____

_____

_____

_____

_____

_____

3. What do words like "sin," "forgiveness," "mercy,"
   and "reconciliation" mean to you?

_____

_____

_____

_____

_____

_____

_____

_____

_____

Today is: _____

Memory Verse or Inspirational Scripture:	Prayer and Thanksgiving for Myself:
My Confessions:	Prayers for Others:

Day ELEVEN

The Blessing of The Thorn

Rushing from my grandmother's house to Memphis for an emergency surgery. It would be the surgery where my doctor placed a trache. I was only 4 years old. Eventually, I was so used to having the trache, I could clean it out myself. Everywhere we went, my mom carried a huge breathing machine, which was extremely loud. She tried to give me the most normal life possible. Every other week, there was a surgery. Even as a child God was equipping me to handle life's challenges without even knowing it.

I never truly realized how different my voice sounded until everyone else started to tell me. It's often easy to cover up flaws with makeup or hair, but what do you do when your "flaw" can't be covered by anything? It's inevitable to be noticed and even when you try to act "normal", people around you notice your flaw. Our afflictions are often our biggest blessings. Your "thorn" may not necessarily be a physical flaw. Your thorn could possibly be someone leaving your life, then God replacing that person with your soulmate or failing a test you really wanted to pass, but getting into law school anyway. In the end, the "thorn" can actually be a blessing.

I've had to overcome many thorns in life in order to realize my blessings. At one point, I felt that having my children out of wedlock were a thorn. My sin was something that I couldn't hide behind closed doors. It was obvious I had children without being married, Everyone knew I was very young with children who were headed to middle school. Anyone with a little common sense would know the timing didn't add up unless I had them as a teenager. I was embarrassed, but more so for my children. Feeling bad because I feel like I stripped my children of a normal life because of my mistakes in the past. Would they ever be able to experience having a father figure in their life? Would they ever see me get married and reach my personal goals? I beat myself up for so long about my mistakes in life.

I was never ashamed of them, but ashamed of my poor decisions in life, which only made my life harder. But then I heard the Lord say, "How many souls are we losing because we are silent about our suffering? Are you humble enough to admit that you messed up in the first place?" I felt my sin was different because people could see it. How many souls were I holding hostage by sweeping my past under the rug? In order to reach my destiny, I had to be honest about my downfalls, my imperfections, my mistakes. God made motherhood my ministry.

I couldn't lie and pretend like I never committed the sin. So how would you look at sin if it was obvious to others that you did it? You couldn't hide it? Some things you can't ignore, so you have to just face it. Even when I decided to completely walk in my testimony, follow Jesus with my whole heart, I faced many trials. Many people doubted that I had changed, I was talked about and persecuted for my past. Making the sacrifice is hard, but in the end you will see a return in your investment. Persecution is inevitable when you decide to follow Christ. Your life will not be easy and everyday won't be happy, but you will be blessed in the midst of hurt. You will conquer in the middle of confusion and in the end your rewards of eternal life with Jesus will be an amazing reward. The glory on the other side of your heartbreak, pain, persecution and feeling of emptiness outweighs the pain in any moment. Don't allow yourself to be so consumed with your troubles that you miss out on the blessings in the midst of your debris.

Scripture Reading:

2 Corinthians 12:7b-9 (NIV)

Therefore, in order to keep me from becoming conceited, I was given a thorn in my flesh, a messenger of Satan, to torment me. Three times I pleaded with the Lord to take it away from me. But he said to me, "My grace is sufficient for you, for my power is made perfect in weakness."

Devotional Reading:

Roses are beautiful flowers. They signify anything from love and gratitude to friendship and new starts, depending on the color. Roses smell beautiful. The aroma of a fresh vase of roses fills the room with an unmistakable pleasant fragrance that sends the recipient into a trance of bliss. But, one aspect of the rose comes across as negative and hurtful, the thorns. For most varieties of roses, the only way to miss the thorns is to do without the flower and the fragrance. Because of the beauty of the petals and the glory of the aroma, we put up with the pain of the thorns. Life has thorns, too. Sure, life has spectacular flowers and the blessing of the scent. But along the journey of life, thorns will invariably arise. In 2 Corinthians 12, the Apostle Paul teaches us some lessons about how thorns can actually be a blessing in our lives.

Lesson #1: Thorns help combat pride.

Pride is a dangerous trait that is difficult to overcome. Paul said that the thorn in his flesh kept him from becoming conceited. When we have everything in our lives under control, we tend to become arrogant with the thought that we can handle anything. The thorn forced Paul to realize that there are many things in life that he could not control. Paul could not radiate conceit when the dreaded thorn reared its ugly head. The thorns in our lives teach us humility. Because arrogance can be such a debilitating flaw in our walk with the Lord, the pride-controlling thorn is a blessing.

Lesson #2: Thorns may be here to stay.

On three different occasions, Paul begged the Lord to take the thorn in the flesh away. God refused. There are going to be some thorns in our lives that God chooses to leave rather than take away. When God says "no" to our cry for Him to take away the thorn, we have to trust the

Lord that our relationship with Him is stronger with the thorn present than with the thorn absent.

Lesson #3: Thorns teach us to trust Christ more.

Thorns highlight the weakness in our life. Thorns reveal how desperately we need the strength of the Lord. Thorns teach us how to rely on Christ to get us through and carry us on. Because the thorn is too much for me to handle, I learn that I must trust Him to handle it. The great news is Jesus promises that His "grace is sufficient." The grace of God in our lives will be more than enough to live with the thorn. Thorns give God's grace the opportunity to pour into our lives.

Because of the blessings that thorns bring into our lives, we can actually thank God for the thorns. Without the thorns, we would miss out on the blooms of life. And God promises to provide everything we need to handle the thorn. Learn to trust the end result of the bouquet in the vase and let God handle the thorns in your life along the way. Ultimately, they will be a blessing.

Devotional Questions

1. Have you ever thanked God for the thorns in your life?

_____

_____

_____

_____

_____

_____

_____

_____

2. What are the thorns in your life and how have your thorns catapulted you into your destiny?

_____

_____

_____

_____

_____

_____

_____

_____

3. Explain how you can see your thorns from God's point of view. Provide Bible Scriptures to support your answer.

_____

_____

_____

_____

_____

_____

_____

_____

_____

_____

_____

_____

_____

_____

_____

_____

Today is: _____

Memory Verse or Inspirational Scripture:	Prayer and Thanksgiving for Myself:
My Confessions:	Prayers for Others:

Day TWELVE

Glam

After I rededicated my life to God, I started to slowly change everything about myself in order to please God. Many times, people have reached out to me asking for prayer, telling me they love my style, personality and testimony. The compliments became repetitive and I started to wonder how and why people saw so many great things in me. I slowly began to share pieces on my testimony and I would always get the same reaction, "I would have never guessed you've been through all of that."

You see, many people see your "glam". They see you after you've been through hell, they see you after you've managed to seek God and pull your life together, but often times, people don't get to see that God's grace and mercy are what has brought you this far. God is so faithful. His mercy endures forever and his grace is sufficient. Imagine if we looked like all we had been through. Imagine if God gave us what we really deserved. We all would be a mess. God's Love And Mercy encompasses any mistakes that we've done. His love and mercy overshadows every single time the world doubted us. It engulfs every piece of gossip that could slander your reputation, because in Him we are made new.

Until a yes from Jesus is enough for you you'll never be fully satisfies or able to walk into your destiny! Man can't destroy you! Man can't take away what God has given you! There is power in fully surrendering to God! The very thing you're praying for may be what God is preparing you for! You may see the glam, but you must know that the battle behind the beauty is more powerful than anything else! God knows what you can handle and he is preparing you through each and every test in your life! You can dress up your mess, but God sees the heart!

Scripture Reading:
1 Timothy 4:8 (NIV)
For physical training is of some value, but godliness has value for all things, holding promise for both the present life and the life to come.

Devotional Reading:
When people see me, they see the outer part of who I am. They see the put-together me. They see the "Glam." But, what they don't see is the hurt, pain, struggle, and

abuse that I have been through. They don't see the internal scars. They don't see the weight of a past that is less than perfect and has been through too much to describe. It is not so much that the glam hides all that I have been through, but that even with all I have been through, the glam can be there at all. How does that happen? How can I have any glam with my past experiences? The answer to that is simple: God's Love and Mercy.

God's love is displayed so clearly in His grace that He pours into my life. Even with my past imperfections and pains, God loves me. In fact, He has loved we through all of it and hurt along with me in the midst of it. But when His grace is poured out lavishly on my life, then all of the hurts and pain can be healed and the joy of knowing Him can shine through. I want people to see the end result of God's grace in me. I want to look good and look happy. I want the people to notice the glam. But this is not an effort to pretend to be something I'm not. It is an effort to point to how great God's grace is in our lives and how He can take even the worst of situations and the worst experiences in my life and help me overcome them to His glory. My glam is not a testament to how strong I am. It is evidence of how great God's grace is. I want people to see His grace in me.

God's grace is partnered with God's mercy in my life. God's mercy has withheld from me the deserved effects of God's wrath so that the love of God can be prominently displayed in me. God's mercy doesn't let me go when everyone else in the world has given up on me. God's mercy doesn't give up on me. His mercy works to highlight His faithful love and concern for me. It is through God's mercy that I can show the end results of healing and restoration. That is what is seen in me. But, it is only possible because of His mercy.

So, in my life, "GLAM" has taken on a whole new meaning. The restoration and healing of a loving, grace-filled, merciful God has allowed the goodness of God to shine through in my life. The GLAM that is the end result brings the godliness that "has value for all things, holding promise for both the present life and the life to come" (see verse above). God has done that in me.

Don't be fooled by the glam that you see. That is not who I am making myself to be. It is who God has made and is making me to be. And, it is only possible because of God's Love And Mercy. That is my GLAM!

Devotional Questions

1. What worldly desire has God taken away from you?

_____

_____

_____

_____

_____

_____

_____

_____

2. Reflect on a specific time or time(s) where God's Love and Mercy shined bright within your life, even when you may not have deserved it.

_____

_____

_____

_____

_____

_____

_____

_____

_____

_____

_____

_____

_____

_____

3. What are you giving up that pleases your flesh, but
    dishonors God? Why? (Elaborate with scripture)

_____

_____

_____

_____

_____

_____

_____

_____

_____

_____

_____

_____

Day THIRTEEN
You Are Not Alone

There isn't anything that you can do to remove yourself from the love of Jesus Christ. You may not be able to speak eloquently through prayer. You may not be able to memorize each bible verse from front to back. Your skirt may not swing past your ankles and your singing voice may literally be nothing but a mess of joyful NOISE, but God still can work through you. You're never too messed up for Jesus Christ.

Every relationship I have ever been in, except for two have been abusive. I've experienced being slapped and hit by men who said they loved me. I have experienced being called every derogatory name during simple arguments. I've had men tell me that nobody would ever love me with two kids and that I should just settle. I've had people who scream they love me, only to look at me and tell me that they wish I would die. It has been hard to come to grips with the fact that a relationship or friendship that isn't God centered will always be tumultuous. I was so embarrassed to reveal to others the things that I had gone through, because it's so easy to smile and allow people to think you have it all together, but nobody really does.

God is never far away from you. I felt lonely when I was going through all of these situations, because I was too ashamed to tell someone that I was hurting, so I dealt with my pain in silence. Eventually, I got the help that I needed from counselors and books and deep prayer. I prayed for healing, because not only was I tired of being hurt and broken but I was tired of pretending to be okay. I knew that if I never healed from my pain, I would never be able to properly love the people around me.

I spent many years avoiding God, because I felt that I didn't fit in. I wasn't talented enough. I didn't know how to sing, dance or do much else that could benefit the kingdom (or so I thought). I felt that other people's convictions were my own obligation. I felt that I wasn't welcomed in God's kingdom because my life wasn't perfect. I was completely wrong. Learning to love your process can help you heal from any mistake you've made in your life. God has and will always be waiting for a yes from you with open arms. The body of Christ can often seem small, but we need each other.

You Are Not Alone

Scripture Reading:

Deuteronomy 31:6 (NIV)

"Be strong and courageous. Do not be afraid or terrified because of them, for the Lord your God goes with you; he will never leave you nor forsake you."

Devotional Reading:

Loneliness is a heavy burden to bear. And, loneliness is an epidemic in our society. Interestingly, in a time when we are the most connected through Facebook, Instagram, emails, texts, Skype, and even the old-fashioned phone call, there are more lonely people around us than ever. Maybe you are one of those lonely people. Though we know more about what is going on in each other's lives through those digital ways of connecting, we actually are more disconnected than we have ever been. Digital relationships give us a false sense of connectedness. On our phone apps, we deal with each other for just a moment then move on to the next digital nugget of information or the next digital friend. When we are talking face to face, we do not move on to the next item nearly as quickly, and we are forced to observe what the other person is saying rather than reading a few lines and moving along. In our most connected world, we have more people disconnected than ever. They feel alone. They are lonely. Is that you?

You need to hear the truth of the Scripture you read above: "the Lord your God goes with you." God is with you. There is never a time when you step out of the presence of God. The marvelous truth of the Bible is that you are never alone. You may feel alone, but you are not alone. God is with you. He is always with you. Whatever you are going through right now, you are not alone. God is with you. When you feel like no one else in the world knows you or knows what you are facing, you are not alone. God is with you. When you have no one that gets you or cares about you, you are not alone. God is with you. Even in the Christian walk it often seems lonely. You think that no one else in the world is there for you. Trust what God says in His word: you are not alone. God is with you.

You also need to hear a second truth that you read in the Scripture above: "He will never leave you nor forsake you." Not only is God with you, He is never leaving you. He will always be with you. And, He will never forsake you. To forsake something or someone is to abandon them, to give up on them, to turn away from them. God says that He will never forsake you. He will never abandon, give up on, or turn away from you. His presence will always be with you, and He will always be on your side. God wants what is best for you. He is looking out for your best interests. He is doing that which will be the absolute best for you when everything is said and done.

In the midst of your loneliness, don't miss this truth: God is with you, He loves you, and He has not given up on you or abandoned you. You are not alone!

Devotional Questions

1. What kind of people do you think of when you think of **lonely** people?

_____

_____

_____

_____

_____

_____

_____

_____

_____

_____

_____

_____

_____

_____

_____

_____

2. What is the most important relationship in your life?

_____

_____

_____

_____

_____

_____

_____

_____

3. What opportunities do you have to open up your life to others in the church?

_____

_____

_____

_____

Day FOURTEEN
Overcoming Abuse and Hurt

Serial dater.

That's the only word that could describe me.

I love the idea of love. I've been in relationships with the worst of the worse. Mentally abusive, physically abusive, cheaters, rapist. You name it. No exaggeration. My issues stemmed from viewing my adoption as being unloved by my biological mother. I always felt like I wasn't good enough for my biological mother. My mother loves me unconditionally. She would give her life for me, but I always wondered why my biological mother didn't want me. I was touched by my step brother before I was even 7. And at 15, I was raped by my "boyfriend", who is now the estranged father of my two children. My journey to SELF LOVE has been an extreme one. I've been judged, made fun of, talked about and many things I'm revealing...nobody else knows.

When we search for "ourselves" through the opinions of other, we have put ourselves in a prison by believing our worth is determined by the validation from people. Until we

realize that God approves of whom we are, what we are,
and what we are capable of doing as His children, only
then we will break the chains we've put on our own lives.

I've even had to overcome self- destruction. I was
dying, physically, mentally and emotionally until Jesus
rescued me. Self-destruction embodied everything in my
life. I could not rule my own world and live a meaningful
life at the same time. I was ruled by alcohol and sexual
immorality. I was a thief, a liar and a quitter. The decaying
effects of resentment, selfishness and arrogance showed in
every aspect of my life. With my own hands, I didn't
realize that I was on the verge of destroying everything
God set up for me.

After many nights of desperate cries to the Lord, He
set me free. God spoke to me and led me straight back to
Him. I had no other choice, because I couldn't handle life
on my own. Jesus paid a price to save us. He created us all
for a specific purpose. He is powerful enough to heal us
and our broken pieces. He is powerful enough to forgive
our transgression. Only He can give us a new start and a
renewed spirit. The same way God delivered me from the
shackles of the enemy, he can do the same for you. I was

lost, but now I'm complete and whole. Today I am living the abundant life and all glory goes to the King of Kings!

Being an Overcomer

Scripture Reading:

Psalm 34:17-18 (NIV)

The righteous cry out, and the Lord hears them; he delivers them from all their troubles. The Lord is close to the brokenhearted and saves those who are crushed in spirit.

Devotional Reading:

Most people have things in the past that they wished had not happened. Most of those are regrets from poor decisions or wrong turns taken in life. But some carry the emotional, or even physical, scars of abuse where someone else has inflicted pain and cruelty on them. Please hear this word of hope: In Christ, you can overcome those experiences and the baggage that you carry from those experiences. They do not have to define you are dictate your direction in life. You can be an overcomer.

If your heart still aches over the way someone mistreated you, here is a roadmap to seeking relief from that heartbreak. First, you must know where to go. People go to many different places and try many different things to get the relief that they seek. Some go to the bottle. Others go to unhealthy relationships. Still others pour themselves into their work at the cost of everything else in life. And others just crawl into a hole of depression and don't see any way out. You may have tried some or even all of these to try and stop the hurting in your heart. The only place to go that can bring the healing that you seek is Jesus. Psalm 34:17 promises that the Lord hears your cry. He knows your hurt. He longs to heal you. But, you must come to Him. Stop trying to self-medicate through other avenues and run to the embrace of the Savior who loves you. Healing is found nowhere else but Jesus.

After knowing where to go, know what to do when you get there. You have to receive the healing that Jesus is offering. You have to trust Him to do the work in you that can bring the restoration that you seek. You have to answer the question: "Do you want to get well?" (See John 5:6.) Some people have been hurting so long that they have become attached to the misery of carrying the scars. Jesus can free you from that. But, you have to want to be made whole. When you come to Jesus, let Him do His healing work in you.

Finally, when you know where to go and what to do, trust the Lord with the final outcome. Romans 8:28 tells us that "in all things God works for the good of those who love him" (NIV). Hear this clearly: it is not that all things are good that happen to us in life. Some things are wrong and evil and bad. You have experienced some of those things. But even in the bad things, the abuse you have experienced, God can turn that bad and bring something good out of it. Maybe He will use you to minister to others. Maybe He will use it so that you can trust Him more. Maybe your speaking out will save others from experiencing the same thing. God can bring about good even in your darkest bad.

God is a God who heals. Will you let Him heal you and then use you as He makes you an overcomer of the abuse you have suffered? Let Him do that in you.

Devotional Questions

1. What comfort can you find in knowing that God will protect and guide you during any difficult time?

    _____

    _____

    _____

_____

_____

_____

_____

_____

_____

_____

2. Consider what you have lost in the middle of heartache and tragedy. As you acknowledge the emotions you are working through, you may be able to find comfort in the following Scriptures:

- The death of a loved one: Matthew 5:4; 2 Corinthians 5:8; Psalm 116:15
- Ilness: Matthew 26:39; Psalm 103:3; Isaiah 53:5; Jeremiah 17:14
- The separation of family members: Ephesians 3:20
- The loss of a job: Philippians 4:19; Matthew 6:31-34
- Financial troubles: Psalm 34:10; Joshua 1:8; Luke 6:38

Notes

Today is: _____

Memory Verse or Inspirational Scripture:	Prayer and Thanksgiving for Myself:
My Confessions:	Prayers for Others:

Day FIFTEEN

Thou Shall Change The Game

When I finally gave my life to Christ, I struggled because I felt like I didn't fit in with the world, but I also felt that I didn't fit in with other Christians. Everyone around me and on social media seemed perfect, but here I was, a broken girl who had made so many senseless mistakes in life. I was doing so many things that God had told me to do, but my story still didn't look like any of my sisters in Christ. I watched so many sisters move to new and exciting places, but God told me to stay where I was. I saw so many sisters meet great men of God and end up engaged within months, but my love story just wasn't happening that quickly. I struggled with comparison and it was making me miserable.

I had to learn that just because God hadn't called me to do the same things others are called to do, it didn't mean that I was any less loved by God. Just because everyone else seemed to be getting married and living the "dream" life didn't mean that God wasn't behind the scenes making my very own dream life come true. You must understand that if one sister or brother in Christ is being blessed, then surely this is proof that God never stops working. He never takes a day off and in due time your season is on the way. God doesn't work on our time. The tears you've sown will not come back void. God has heard every prayer, every cry and he has collected them in all of his Glory and he will bring forth the promises of His word. You are worthy. You deserve the best. When you fully surrender to God, he will make things that seem impossible, happen.

Today, I'm at a point in my life where I never ever thought I would be. The same voice I was ashamed of is used to speak in front of thousands to tell my testimony. I used to avoid anything teen pregnancy related, but I volunteer my time to work, bless and speak to teen girls about following their dreams, abstinence and how to pick up the pieces of life after you've made mistakes. God is so faithful. The very things that you're afraid of, will end up being what God uses for you to help someone else breakthrough. I don't necessarily have the typical look of what people would say a Christian should be. I am loud when you get to know me. I love my hair way down my back or big and curly. I wear bright colors and my past isn't pretty, but God is perfect.

When I first began to share my testimony, people judged me. The enemy knows what God has put inside of you. The enemy will use whatever and whoever he can to stop you from fulfilling God's plan. I prayed for years before obeying God's calling on my life and he gave me the courage to keep going even when I had no idea what I was doing. I know that although many people have laughed at me and doubted me, because of my past, there are people who believed in the God in me. I'm encouraging you to keep going even when the world is against you, because God is with you.

God doesn't call those who are perfect and although those around you may seem perfect, everyone has their own struggles and convictions. You're not alone in any aspect of this journey. Your life is your ministry. Your mistakes have molded you into the person God need you to be in order to fulfill his mission. You're never "in too deep" to be rescued by the Savior. Your failures have activated your faith. You can do all things through Christ, who strengthens you. I pray this short journey through the debris of my mistakes in life, has shown you that God can and will use anybody....even you. God Bless.

You Can Change the World!

Scripture Reading:

Philippians 1:6 (NIV)

Being confident of this, that he who began a good work in you will carry it on to completion until the day of Christ Jesus.

Devotional Reading:

Artists amaze me. They sit in front of a blank canvas and see the end result of the painting before they even put one drop of paint on the brush. Then, they bring to life what they have already seen in their mind. For great artists, the end result is inspiring and amazing. Similarly, God looked at the blank canvas of your life and saw the end product before He started doing the work on your heart. And, as you just read in the verse above, that which God has started, He will complete in your life. He's not through working on you, and He's not through using you. God is going to use you to change the world!

You may be already making excuses as to why God can't use you to change the world. Those excuses make the huge mistake of underestimating what God can do and the lengths to which He will go to use you in a mighty way in this world. Let's work at shooting down the excuses that keep you from being all that God has saved you to be.

I'm Too Messed Up

Many think: "God can't use me. I've made mammoth mistakes and have fallen way short of what God wants in me. My flaws are numerous and debilitating. I'm too messed up for God to use." The Lord longs for you to let Him bring healing to your brokenness. Let Him bring restoration to your mistakes. Let Him bring forgiveness to you sin. God's grace is available and abundant to cover all of the messes in your life. You are not too far gone to be rescued by the Savior. Psalm 51 is King David's reaction to his sin of adultery with Bathsheba and of murder with Uriah. When God uncovers David's sin and brings conviction to his heart, David cries for the merciful God to rain down grace into his life. Then, David says: "Then I will teach transgressors your ways, so that sinners will turn back to you" (Psalm 51:13, NIV). David is saying that after God has cleansed him from the sins of murder and adultery, David could make a difference in the world around him. The adulterer and murderer was not too messed up to be used of God. Neither are you.

I'm Useless

Some say that they don't bring anything of value to the table that God can use. If God created you and saved you, then He has placed in you much value for doing His kingdom work. God doesn't call the most talented, most beautiful, or the most popular. He calls the small, weak things of the world to do great things for Him. "But God chose the foolish things of the world to shame the wise; God chose the weak things of the world to shame the strong" (1 Corinthians 1:27, NIV). God uses those who think they are useless to change the world.

I'm Scared

Some people are simply too scared to step up and do what God calls them to do. Listen to these words: "I can do all this through him who gives me strength" (Philippians 4:13). Christ wants to do great things through you. He will do the work. He will make it happen. He just wants you to be available to be used by Him. It is not a question of you being able to do it. The question is if you will trust the Lord to do it through you.

We have taken a journey through the debris of my mistakes in life. Through it all my prayer is that God has revealed to you that He can and will use anyone...even you. God wants to use you to change the world.

Devotional Questions

1. How can we be confident in the fact that the good work that God began in us "will carry on to completion"?

_____

_____

_____

_____

_____

_____

_____

_____

_____

_____

_____

_____

_____

_____

_____

_____

_____

_____

2. What is the relationship between this confidence
   and the joy that you should strive to maintain in
   your life?

   _____

   _____

   _____

   _____

   _____

   _____

   _____

   _____

   _____

   _____

   _____

Today is: _____

Memory Verse or Inspirational Scripture:	Prayer and Thanksgiving for Myself:
My Confessions:	Prayers for Others:

Made in the USA
Middletown, DE
07 April 2020

88243285R00080